Pledge of ALLEGIANCE

EUGENE HARRIS (USMC RET)

ISBN 978-1-64515-007-7 (paperback)
ISBN 978-1-64515-008-4 (digital)

Christian Faith Publishing, Inc.
832 Park Avenue
Meadville, PA 16335
www.christianfaithpublishing.com

All scripture is from the King James Version unless otherwise noted.

Printed in the United States of America

INTRODUCTION

After the tragedy that took place on September 11, 2001, our country has undergone some changes, some good and some bad. People has rallied around "God Bless America" while other want to disband the Pledge of Allegiance. God has already blessed America; it is up to American people to receive the finished work. There are people who think that by making a pledge of allegiance is against their constitutional rights, so to justify their thinking, they want the pledge to be withdrawn from our public school system. Both you and I have recited the Pledge of Allegiance over and over during our school years and can recite it without thinking about it. How many of us has really sat down and thought about the Pledge of Allegiance? Why do we recite it? What does it really means? These questions were addressed to a youth group ages six to twelve, and not one of the students really knew what the Pledge of Allegiance was about. Yes, they all could recite it but didn't know its origin or meaning. If these young people didn't know, how many more others that doesn't know?

THE PLEDGE OF ALLEGIANCE

I pledge allegiance to the flag of the United States of America and to the republic for which it stands one nation under God indivisible with liberty and justice for all.

THE PLEDGE OF ALLEGIANCE

(A Short History)

Francis Bellamy (1855–1931), a Baptist minister, wrote the original Pledge in August 1892. He was a Christian Socialist. In his Pledge, he is expressing author of the American socialist utopian novels, *Looking Backward* (1888) and *Equality* (1897) the ideas of his first cousin, Edward Bellamy.

His original Pledge read as follows: "I pledge allegiance to my Flag and (to)[1] the Republic, for which it stands, one nation, indivisible, with liberty and justice for all." He considered placing the word "equality" in his Pledge but knew that the state superintendents of education on his committee were against equality for women and African Americans.

---

[1] "to" added in October 1892

In 1923 and 1924 the National Flag Conference, under the leadership of the American Legion and the Daughters of the American Revolution, changed the Pledge's words "my Flag" to "the Flag of the United States of America."

In 1954, Congress, after a campaign by the Knights of Columbus, added the words "under God" to the Pledge. The Pledge was now both a patriotic oath and a public prayer. We as a nation do stand square on the doctrine of liberty and justice for all.

Country

Our country was founded and established on God's word and his principles. We see throughout the Bible the focus on establishing a nation (a people) that is centered around God. Since the Pledge of Allegiance was instituted as a public prayer and a patriotic oath, we can see clearly why the United States of America is a blessed nation. Now after all these years of being a standard opening of every schoolchild's day,

the Pledge of Allegiance is now being ide. as unconstitutional. Let us example the United States of America from the content on wh was based on—God's word.

Our Pledge

"I"

Represent an individual person (not a group). It involves a person's will, a will to stand up and be counted, regardless of the opposition. I have the right to excise the power of choice.

"Pledge"

Is one of commitment, to make a vow or pledge with wiliness to keep it. The Scripture teaches us that a man's word is more honorable than his name (God hold his word above his name). When you make a vow to God or man, do not delay to pay it or keep it for it is better not to vow (pledge) than to do so and not keep it. Do not let your mouth cause your body to sin. In other words, don't allow yourself to be labeled as one who lacks integrity.

"Allegiance"

To aid and come in agreement with; your interest is my interest. The motto for one of our finest military institution (West Point) learns duty, honor, and country, a promise to continue a relationship. It is the allegiance that made our country free. "A false balance is abomination to the Lord: but a just weight is his delight" (Gideon's International).

"To the Flag of the United States of America"

Flag represents the people. The Constitution states, *"We the people of the United States."* The flag is a symbol/banner that all can identify with. The Red, White, and Blue has God's signature—red (the blood he shed to redeem man), white (purity of his holiness), blue (justice, the righteousness of his person). Our military calls the flag a standard one of authority and power (when the enemy comes in like a flood, the Spirit of the Lord will rise up a standard against him),

God's authority and power. Our flag stands for united, union, and unity of the people.

"Republic (for which it stands)"

A Republic is a form of government operating on principles adopted from a republic and democracy. We are a nation, a proud people, and when the chips are down, we all raise to the occasion. Throughout our country's history (good or bad), we still function as one, a concern for all people.

"One Nation under God"

"Under" is to say we are submitted to the authority of that which we claim and that is a nation under God. This nation will say what God said. This is evidence by the inscription at the foot of the Statue of Liberty: "Give me your tired, your poor, your huddled masses yearning to breathe free, the wretched refuse of your teeming shore. Send these, the homeless, tempest-tost to me; I lift my lamp beside the golden door."

Jesus said it this way, "Come unto me, all ye that labour and heavy laden, and I will give you rest. Take my yoke upon you and learn of me for I am meek and lowly in heart and you shall find rest unto your souls my yoke is easy and my burden is light. I stand at the door and knock. All who open I will come in and sup with him and he with me, and we will be one." If any man (whosoever) call on the name of the Lord shall be save, free. God is in control of a nation that is submitted to him.

"Indivisible"

A house divide against itself cannot stand. Another way of saying we are in covenant with each other. There are several things that the Lord hates, and one is an abomination to him and that is the dividing of the brethrens *paraphrase*. The brethrens are those who have come in agreement with the laws of God and man. Let's look at the United States Armed Force. We see four separated branches but yet one vine (our country). Each has a different mission, but yet it is the same—to protect and defend the Constitution and the American people. Look at the reference scriptures and see if you are incapable of being divided.

"Liberty"

Some may say I have the liberty to express my views and my opinions. But as far as the Pledge of Allegiance goes, this liberty represents freedom (nothing missing and nothing broken). True freedom is found in the word of God. Our forefather recognizes this fact. Our entire country and government system was based on the word of God (after all the word *church* means a governing body). This can be seen in our Constitution, our National Anthem, and our president's addresses (mean it or not), and even our nation mascot, the eagle. Freedom is a gift from a people to a people. Where the Spirit of the Lord is, there is Liberty.

"Justice"

Principle of mortal, rightness, and conduct should not be the focus of just one individual, nor even a group, but on the principle of living right. Noah found grace with God because of his continuous lifestyle of rightness living. Job was perfect (mature), an upright man. Job was a righteous dude. Many times people have cried out because they feel that justice has escaped them for one reason nor another. Well, I will leave you with this one thought from my big brother: "If you do well, will you not be accepted?"

"All"

Total entity or extent of; everything being taking into account. The Bible said "whosoever." That is you and me, white, black, yellow, red, brown, and if there are some purple people out there, that goes for you too. God so loved the world (the people) that he (God) gave his only begotten son, that through his son we may all have an allegiance with God. God bless America.

FROM THE AUTHOR

As Americans we are responsible to each other and most of all to God. There is no excuse for ignorance of God's or man's law. I have served my country for over twenty-three years as a United States Marines; from the jungles of Viet Nam to the desert sands of Kuwait. I know first-hand and what it means to be a centurion and to endure hardship. It was an honor to be called an American when I step on foreign shores. I cannot understand that which has held us together now seems meaningless. The Bible tell us, in the book of Ecclesiastes, that there is a time for all things. Now it is time for all good men (women too) to come to the aid of this country. Let us all once again come in agreement that we are one nation, indivisible, with liberty and justice for all.

I Pledge Allegiance (USMC 69-92)

REFERENCE

King James Bible unless otherwise noted.

Pledge: Ecclesiastes 5:5–6

Allegiance: Proverbs 11:1 (Gideon's International); Genesis 15:18; Joshua 24:15; Psalm23:6, 37:5;
John17:21

Flag: Isaiah 59:19, Genesis 11:6, Acts 2:1, Psalm 133:1

Republic: Acts 4:32–34

One Nation: Genesis 1:1; John1:1–2; Psalm 23:1, 119:89; Proverbs 3:5–6; Psalm 33:12

Indivisible: Amos 3:3; Proverbs 6:16–19, 25:19; John17:21; 2 Thessalonians 3:6; Psalm 125:1; Matthew 11:28–30; Romans 10:13; Revelations 3:20

Liberty: Luke 4:18, 2 Corinthians 3:17

Justice: Genesis 4:7, 6:9; Job1:8

ABOUT THE AUTHOR

Eugene Harris was born in Columbus, Georgia, on October 23, 1950, and move with his family to Detroit, Michigan, at a young age. Eugene was educated in Detroit, Michigan, and graduated from Northern High School in January 1969. After high school, he attended college at Detroit Institute of Technology (DIT) for one semester before joining the United States Marines Corps in July of the same year. Eugene received all military training in California before shipping out to Vietnam.

In September 1970 he was discharge from the Marines Corps because of the wounds he received in Vietnam, after eighteen months of rehabilitation, he was back on active duty. Eugene retired from active duty in June 1992 with twenty-three years of honorable service. He received several personal and campaign medals over his career, and to this day he is still a Marine at heart.

After retirement Eugene went back to college and received two college degrees: AAS Computer Aided Design and BS in Business Information Systems as well as several certifications. He worked for twenty-one years in the engineering field until his retirement in July of 2017. He lives in Temecula, California, with his wife Beatrice and has two daughters from a previous marriage, Eugenia and Regina, both in Detroit, Michigan, (two daughter are decease: Sharlitta and Tangela); a daughter by marriage, Patrice Reitz of Williamsport, Pennsylvania; and several grandchildren and great-grandchildren.

There are several things that the Marine Corps has taught Eugene, and the most important one was their motto "Semper Fidelis," a Latin phrase that's means, "Always Faithful" or "Always Loyal." "Yes, we as Americans have our ups and downs, but I will never turn my back on her nor our flag or the principle for which we stand by. Doing so would mean turning our back on God," says Eugene. "Let us continue to believe in American and let's stay united."

www.ingramcontent.com/pod-product-compliance
Lightning Source LLC
Chambersburg PA
CBHW051429250726
48655CB00003B/1321